EVERYDAY HEALTHY

40 family recipes

SOUPS & SIDES

PASTA & RICE

MAINS

DESSERTS

SOUPS & SIDES

FENNEL AND BACON SOUP

Melt the butter in the stockpot over medium heat. Add the sliced leeks and cook gently for 10 minutes, stirring occasionally, until soft. Stir in the chopped fennel and potatoes. Pour in the stock and bring to a boil. Cover and simmer for 30 minutes. Stir in the cream and season to taste with salt and pepper.

Preheat a frying pan over medium heat. Add the pancetta or bacon and fry for 3-4 minutes until crispy. Ladle the soup into bowls and top with the bacon and some fresh thyme leaves.

60 MIN

- 2 tbsp butter
- 2 large leeks (sliced)
- 2 fennel bulbs (coarsely chopped)
- 6 cups hot chicken broth
- 2 potatoes (roughly chopped)
- ½ cup non-fat cream
- Handful fresh thyme leaves (roughly chopped)
- 4 slices of pancetta or smoked bacon
- Salt and pepper

- 2 tbsp butter
- 1 onion (chopped)
- 2 lb pumpkin or
  butternut squash (deseeded and cubed)
- 2 garlic cloves (crushed)
- 4 tbs low fat cream
- 6 cups hot vegetable broth
- 4 tbsp shaved Parmesan
- A pinch of curry powder
- 2 bay leaves
- Small bunch of fresh cilantro
- Salt and pepper

PUMPKIN & PARMESAN SOUP

Melt the butter in the casserole over medium to low heat. Add the onion and pumpkin and sauté, stirring for 5 minutes. Add the garlic and bay leaves and cook, stirring for an additional 5 minutes. Add the stock. Increase the heat, bringing the soup to a boil, then simmer for 10 minutes or until the pumpkin is soft. Remove the bay leaves.

Purée the soup using a blender until smooth. Return the casserole to low heat and stir in the cream. Season to taste with curry powder, salt and pepper. Serve with a few slivers of Parmesan and some coriander leaves.

CHICKEN NOODLE SOUP

- 2 chicken breasts
- 9 cups water
- 1 large onion (cut in half)
- 1 large garlic clove (cut in half)
- ½ inch piece fresh ginger (peeled and sliced)
- 2 celery stalks (chopped)
- 1 leek (chopped)
- 4 scallions (finely shredded)
- 4 oz egg noodles
- 4 carrots (peeled and shredded)
- 1 bunch fresh cilantro
- Salt and pepper

Put the chicken breasts and water into a stockpot and bring to a boil. Reduce the heat and simmer. Add the onion, garlic, ginger, pepper and salt. Continue to simmer for 20 minutes, or until the chicken is tender and completely cooked. Remove the chicken, the halved onions and garlic. Keep the chicken aside.

Add the celery, leek and scallions to the stock. Bring the stock to a boil, then add the noodles and cook according to the packaging directions. Meanwhile, chop and shred the chicken, add to the pan with the shredded carrot and continue cooking for about one minute. Season to taste with salt and pepper, garnish with chopped fresh cilantro.

 60 MIN

- 2 cups fresh spinach
- 1 tbsp knob of butter
- 1 large onion (finely chopped)
- 2 garlic cloves (chopped)
- ¾ cup feta (crumbled)
- 4 tbsp pine nuts (toasted)
- 3 large free-range eggs (beaten)
- 6 filo pastry sheets
- Salt and pepper

SPINACH AND FETA PIE

Preheat the oven to 350°F. Wilt the spinach in a non-stick pan over low heat. Allow to cool and then drain well, squeezing out all of the excess liquid. Melt the butter in a frying pan and add the onion. Cook for 5 minutes, until soft. Stir in the garlic and cook for another minute.

Remove from the heat and add to a bowl with the spinach, feta, pine nuts and eggs. Mix together and season well. Brush a filo pastry sheet with melted butter, and lay on the bottom of the pie tin. The sheet hangs over the tin, you need the extra ends to fold over the spinach mixture later. Do the same with the other 5 filo sheets and drape them one over the other in the tin.

Spoon in the spinach mixture. Close the pie by folding over the filo sheets, so the whole spinach mixture is covered. Bake in the oven for 25-30 minutes, until the pastry is crisp and golden.

14

THE PERFECT EGG ON TOAST

Put your square egg pan on a medium to low heat and add a drop of oil or butter to lightly coat the bottom. Crack one egg into the pan. Cook until the top of the white is set but the yolk is still runny.

Remove the pan from the heat and slide out the egg on your toast. Serve with a sprinkle of sea salt and freshly ground black pepper.

3 MIN

· 1 egg

· 1 slice of toast

· Salt and pepper

· Oil or butter

MUFFIN TIN BAKED EGGS WITH SALMON

Preheat the oven to 425°F. Take a muffin tin and coat the holes with a bit of butter. Place each of the 6 salmon slices in a muffin hole. Using a spoon fill the holes with the beaten eggs. Sprinkle the black pepper on top.

Eggs with salmon

· 5 eggs (beaten)

· 6 slices of salmon

· Butter

· Fresh parsley to garnish

Bacon & eggs

· 6 bacon slices

· 6 eggs

· Salt and pepper

BACON & EGGS

In the 6 other muffin holes place a slice of bacon. Break an egg into the bacon. Sprinkle with some black pepper. Place the muffin tin with salmon eggs and bacon eggs in the oven for about 12 minutes. When done take them out using a silicone palette and serve hot.

 20 MIN 6

- 4 tsp fresh yeast or
  2 tsp dried yeast

- 3 tsp sugar

- 1 ⅓ cup water

- 4 cups bread flour,
  plus extra for dusting

- 3 tsp salt

- 2 cups cherry tomatoes

- 1 cup black olives

- 10 tbsp extra-virgin olive oil

- Some fresh rosemary sprigs

- Sea salt and freshly ground black pepper

FOCACCIA

Dissolve the sugar in half the tepid water. On a clean surface or in a large bowl, make a pile of the flour and salt. Make a well in the centre and pour in all the dissolved yeast. Slowly bring in more and more of the flour until all the yeast mixture is soaked up. Then pour the other 1/2 of the tepid water into the centre and gradually incorporate all the flour to make a moist dough.

Roll, push and fold the dough over and over for 5 minutes. Flour your hands, and lightly flour the top of the dough. Make it into a roundish shape and place it on a baking tray. Let rest and double in size in a warm space. This should take around 40 minutes. Take the proofed dough and bash the air out, then put it on a floured surface and roll it out about 1 inch thick. Transfer it to a floured baking tray and push the dough to fill the tray.

Push your fingers to the bottom of the tray across the whole dough. This gives the bread a classic shape and makes indentations so you get little pools of oil while it's baking. Leave to proof until it has doubled in size again then sprinkle with salt and pepper and carefully place into a preheated oven at 425°F. Bake for 20 minutes, until the bread is crisp and golden on top and soft in the middle.

Pour over the olive oil and push in the tomatoes and olives and sprinkle over the rosemary.

 70 MIN

- 4 cups plain flour
- 1 egg yolk
- 6 ¾ tsp fresh yeast or
  2 ¼ tsp dry yeast
- 3 tbsp olive oil
- 1 cup lukewarm water
- ½ lb pepperoni
- 1 onion (thin sliced)
- 1½ cups tomato sauce
- 4 cups grated cheese
- Salt, pepper and dried herbs

PIZZA ROLLS

Preheat the oven to 400°F. Grind the yeast in a large bowl. Pour in lukewarm water and let dissolve. Add the olive oil, egg yolk and mix in the flour and salt.

Work the dough smooth. Let rise 30 minutes. Roll the dough into a large rectangle. If you wish, make 2 smaller rectangles. Brush the dough with tomato sauce and add the pepperoni slices, sliced onion and sprinkle with grated cheese. Gently roll up.

Cut about 24 pieces of 1 inch of the roll. Place pizza rolls upright in a lightly greased muffin pan with the swirled side up. Bake for about 12 minutes.

STRAWBERRY RHUBARB COMPOTE

Combine rhubarb, sugar and lemon juice in a large saucepan. Stir over medium heat until sugar dissolves. Reduce heat to medium-low, cover, and simmer until rhubarb is tender, stirring occasionally, about 4 minutes.

Add strawberries, and simmer for 2-3 minutes, uncovered. Transfer rhubarb mixture to bowl. Cover and chill until cold, about 2 hours.

· 2 cups fresh rhubarb
 (½ inch pieces)
· 2 cups strawberries
 (hulled and chopped)
· 1 ½ cups sugar
· 2 tbsp fresh lemon juice

25

PASTA & RICE

PAELLA

Heat 2 tbsp of the oil in a large frying pan or skillet. Cook the chicken over medium high heat, for about 10 minutes. Transfer them to a large bowl.

Add the chorizo to the pan and cook for 1 minute, then also transfer them to the bowl. Add 2 tbsp oil to the pan and cook the onions, stirring for 2 minutes. Add the garlic and paprika and cook for 3 minutes until the onions are golden. Add the rice and peas and stir well. Return the chicken and chorizo to the pan.

Take a saucepan. Stir the water with the saffron into the stock. Season with salt and pepper and bring to a boil, stirring. Add this stock to the large pan. Reduce the heat and simmer, uncovered, for 15 minutes. Arrange mussels, shrimp and bell peppers on top. Cover and simmer for 7 minutes. Serve immediately. Garnish with fresh parsley.

60 MIN | 161

- 3 tbsp olive oil for frying
- 6 boned chicken thighs
- 4 oz chorizo sausage (sliced)
- 2 onions (chopped)
- 4 garlic cloves (crushed)
- 1 tsp paprika powder
- 2 cups paella or risotto rice
- 1 cup frozen peas
- 6 cups fish stock (made with bouillon cubes)
- ½ tsp saffron threads (soaked in a bit of warm water)
- 16 cleaned mussels (in shell)
- 16 shrimp
- 1 bell pepper (halved and seeded, finely sliced)
- Freshly chopped parsley
- Salt and pepper

PASTA ALLA CARBONARA

- 1 lb linguine
- 6 slices of pancetta
- 1 cup grated Parmesan cheese
- 3 large eggs yolks
- 2 plump garlic cloves (peeled and left whole)
- ¼ cup unsalted butter
- Salt and black pepper

Bring a large casserole of water to a boil. Beat the eggs in a medium bowl, season with a little freshly ground black pepper and set everything aside. Add 1 tsp salt to the boiling water, add the linguine and when the water comes back to a boil, cook at a constant simmer, covered, for 10 minutes or until al dente (just cooked). Crush the garlic with the blade of a knife, just to bruise it.

While the pasta is cooking, drop the butter into a large wide frying pan and fry the pancetta and garlic. Leave these to cook on a medium heat for about 5 minutes, until the pancetta is golden and crisp. Take the garlic out. Keep the heat under the pancetta on low.

When the pasta is ready, drain (keep 1/2 cup of the pasta water!) and lift it with tongs in the frying pan with the pancetta. Mix most of the cheese in with the eggs. Take the pan of linguine and pancetta off the heat. Now quickly pour in the eggs and cheese and, using tongs, lift up the pasta so it mixes easily with the egg mixture, which thickens but doesn't scramble, until everything is coated. Add a few tablespoons pasta cooking water to keep it saucy. Season with a little salt and pepper.

SPRING VEGETABLE RISOTTO WITH SHRIMP

In a shallow bowl, toss the shrimp with the oil, garlic, zest, rosemary, salt and pepper. Let the shrimp marinate at room temperature while you make the risotto. Heat the olive oil in a large sauté pan. Add the onion, fennel and garlic and cook over low heat for about 10 minutes, or until soft and translucent. Season with salt. Add the rice and raise the heat to medium high. Stir to coat and slightly toast the rice for about 3 minutes until the rice will take on a shiny, translucent coat. Add the lemon juice to the rice and continue stirring. Add a ladleful of hot stock to the rice and continue stirring. As the stock is absorbed, continue adding it by ladle and stir. Stop incorporating stock once the rice is creamy but still al dente, cooked but not too soft. This can take between 20 and 30 minutes, and between 6 and 8 cups of stock.

Remove the risotto from the heat, and immediately fold in the butter, mascarpone, preserved lemon rind, peas, pepper and most of the mint (save some for garnish). Stir slowly to blend, check a final time for seasoning, and carefully fold in the asparagus. Put a lid on the risotto and let it rest while you quickly fry the shrimp, for about 1 minute on each side.

Top each serving of risotto with a few shrimp, garnish with mint and serve.

- ¼ cup olive oil
- 2 medium onions (chopped)
- 1 small fennel bulb (chopped)
- 4 cloves garlic (minced)
- 2 cups Arborio rice
- ½ cup lemon juice
- 6-8 cups hot chicken stock
- 3 tbsp unsalted butter
- ½ cup mascarpone
- 2 tbsp lemon rind
- coarsely chopped mint leaves
- 2 cups (frozen) peas
- 1 bunch asparagus (chopped into 2-inch lengths and blanched in salted, boiling water)
- 24 large, deveined shrimp (shell on)
- 3 tbsp olive oil
- 3 cloves of garlic (minced, about 3 tsp.)
- Zest of half a large lemon
- 1 tsp salt
- ½ tsp black pepper

- 1 lb spaghetti

- 2 cloves garlic (for rubbing)

- 2 lemons (zest of 1 lemon, juice of 2 lemons)

- 5 tbsp extra-virgin olive oil

- 1 cup finely grated
  Parmesan cheese (plus extra for sprinkling)

- Bunch fresh flat-leaf parsley

- Salt and pepper

SPAGHETTI AL LIMONE

Place the spaghetti in a pot of boiling salted water and stir immediately to prevent the strands from sticking. Cook the spaghetti to 'al dente' (just cooked follow packaging directions).

Cut the garlic in half and rub the exposed area along the interior of a large serving bowl. The raw garlic flavor will coat the inside surface of the serving bowl. Discard the garlic. Add the freshly squeezed lemon juice and slowly drizzle in extra-virgin olive oil while whisking. Whisk until the ingredients have emulsified. Mix in the salt and Parmesan cheese.

When the spaghetti is 'al dente', drain and add to the serving bowl. Mix the pasta with the lemon sauce to coat evenly. Sprinkle the pasta dish with Parmesan cheese, fresh parsley and lemon zest. Serve immediately.

MAINS

- 2 medium onions (peeled)
- 1 clove of garlic (peeled and crushed)
- 1 medium leek (trimmed)
- ½ fresh red chili (finely chopped)
- 1 tbsp olive oil
- 1 tsp ground cumin
- 1 tsp paprika powder
- 1 tsp dried oregano
- 2 tbsp tomato purée
- 1 can of green lentils (drained and rinsed)
- 1 can of red kidney beans (drained and rinsed)
- 1 can of black beans (drained and rinsed)
- 1 can of chopped tomatoes
- 1 cup vegetable stock
- Fresh coriander leaves
- 1 lime
- Sour cream
- 6 jacket potatoes
- Salt and black pepper

VEGGIE CHILI

Finely chop the onions, garlic, leek and chili and place into a preheated large skillet with the oil. Fry for about 5 minutes, or until softened. Add the spices and dried herbs, then fry for 2 minutes. Stir in the tomato purée and cook for another 2 minutes.

Stir in the lentils, beans and chopped tomatoes, then add the stock. Bring it all to a gentle boil, then reduce to a low heat and let it simmer for 20 minutes. This will taste great on a jacket potato, scattered with coriander leaves and with lime wedges and a dollop of sour cream on the side.

ZUCCHINI SPAGHETTI WITH SALMON

For the marinade: in a bowl, mix the olive oil, garlic, paprika, chili powder and grated lemon rind. Season with salt and pepper. Pour the marinade over the cubed salmon and leave to marinate for a few minutes. In the meantime, use a julienne cutter to slice the zucchini into 'spaghetti'.

Heat the peanut oil in a pan. Sauté the zucchini spaghetti and garlic for 2 minutes, or until transparent. Season with salt and pepper and remove from the pan. Set aside. In the same pan, sauté the salmon for 3 to 4 minutes until tender. Remove the salmon from the pan and briefly sauté the cherry tomatoes. Return all the ingredients to the pan and warm briefly over a high heat. Garnish with fresh basil.

 20 MIN   4

- 1 ½ lbs / 21.3 oz salmon (cubed)
- 2 zucchini
- 1 tbsp peanut oil
- 2 tbsp olive oil
- 7 oz cherry tomatoes (halved)
- Salt and pepper

Marinade

- 2 tbsp olive oil
- 1 clove of garlic (minced)
- Pinch of paprika
- Pinch of chili powder
- ½ organic lemon
- Salt and pepper

Garnish

- Fresh basil

40

- 2 (1 lb) salmon fillets
- 1 lemon
- ¼ tsp sea salt
- ⅛ tsp ground white pepper

HEALTHY STEAMED SALMON

Rinse the fish in cold water and pat dry. Put it in the steamer rack. Sprinkle with sea salt and pepper. Cut half a lemon into slices and put on the fish. Juice the remaining lemon and drizzle over the fish.

Put the steamer rack on top of the sauté pan. Add water in the pan to a depth of 1 inch and bring to a boil. Cover and steam for 8 to 10 minutes.

CHICKEN CURRY IN A HURRY

Heat the oil in a preheated skillet. Add the scallions and stir-fry over medium heat for about 1 minute. Add the curry paste, coconut milk and bouillon and bring gently to a boil.

Add the chicken, half the cilantro and stir. Reduce the heat and simmer for 10 minutes. Garnish with the remaining cilantro and a lime wedge. Serve with cooked rice or noodles.

- 2 tbsp peanut oil
- 5 scallions (chopped)
- 2 tbsp green curry paste
- 3 cups coconut milk
- 1 chicken bouillon cube
- 6 chicken breasts
  (cut into 1-inch cubes)
- Large bunch of fresh chopped cilantro
- 1 lime

HORSERADISH & GRILLED VEGETABLES STEAK

Bring the meat to room temperature. In a small bowl, stir together the sour cream, horseradish, lemon juice and cayenne pepper. Season to taste with salt and pepper and set aside.

In a large bowl, toss the peppers and tomatoes with the olive oil and season generously with salt and pepper. Rub the steaks with salt and pepper. Preheat a grill pan. Add the steaks to the pan and cook until nicely browned underneath, about 3 minutes.

Transfer the peppers and tomatoes to the grill pan and cook, turning occasionally, until softened (in total about 6 minutes). After 3 minutes turn the steaks over and cook until browned on the other side, about 3 minutes for medium-rare. Transfer the steaks to a plate and cover loosely with aluminum foil. Serve with the horseradish sauce and grilled vegetables.

 15 MIN   4

- 4 rib-eye steaks
- 1 cup sour cream
- ¼ cup prepared horseradish
- 1 tbsp fresh lemon juice
- Pinch of cayenne pepper
- 6 gypsy peppers
- 4 plum tomatoes
- Salt and pepper

SLOPPY JOE

Crumble the beef into a large, preheated non-stick skillet; cook over medium heat until it starts to sizzle, about 1 minute. Add onion and peppers and cook, stirring occasionally, breaking up the meat with a wooden spoon, until the vegetables are soft and the moisture has evaporated, for about 10 minutes.

Add tomatoes and flour; stir to combine. Stir in water, vinegar, chili sauce and ketchup and bring to a simmer, stirring often. Reduce heat to a low simmer and cook, stirring occasionally, until the sauce has thickened and the onion is very tender, for about another 10 minutes.

Garnish with some tomato and fresh parsley.

- 1 lb (16 oz) of lean ground beef
- 1 large onion (finely diced)
- 5 tomatoes (dice 3, slice 2)
- 1 green bell pepper
  (seeds and veins removed, minced)
- ½ red bell pepper
  (seeds and veins removed, minced)
- 2 tbsp all-purpose flour
- ½ cup water
- ¼ cup cider vinegar
- ¼ cup chili sauce
- ¼ cup ketchup
- 8 whole-wheat hamburger buns
  (toasted if desired)
- Fresh parsley to garnish

49

Chicken salad

- 2 tbsp olive oil
- 2 chicken breasts (cut into fine strips)
- 1 large cos or romaine lettuce
  (washed, dried and leaves separated)

Dressing

- 1 garlic clove
- 3 anchovies (jar or tin)
- 4 tbsp freshly grated Parmesan cheese
- ⅓ cup mayonnaise
- 1 tbsp white wine vinegar

Croutons

- 4 slices of white bread (cut into small cubes)
- 1 tbsp olive oil
- 2 tbsp butter
- 1 clove garlic (crushed)
- Sea salt and ground black pepper

30 MIN · 4

GRILLED CHICKEN CAESAR SALAD

Rub the chicken strips with some oil, season with salt and pepper. Heat the grill pan over medium heat. Once hot, add the chicken and cook for 4 minutes, then flip. Cook for an additional 4 minutes. Mash the anchovies with a fork against the side of a small bowl. Add the crushed garlic and a handful of grated Parmesan cheese and mix with the mayonnaise and vinegar. Season to taste with pepper. Melt the butter and olive oil in a frying pan on medium heat.

Add a crusted garlic clove and the cubed bread and sauté until they turn golden brown. Put the lettuce in a large bowl.

Cut the chicken into bite-size strips and scatter half over the leaves, along with half the croutons. Add most of the dressing and toss. Scatter the rest of the chicken and croutons, then drizzle with the remaining dressing. Sprinkle Parmesan on top and serve immediately.

FISH NUGGETS

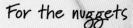

- 1 cup all-purpose flour
- 2 eggs
- 1 cup panko or breadcrumbs
- 1 lb firm white fish fillets
  (Cod, Red Snapper, Pollack...) cut into strips
- 2 tbsp peanut oil
- Salt and pepper

For the light tartar sauce

- ⅔ cup low-fat yogurt
- ¼ cup minced pickles or relish
- 2 tbsp light mayonnaise
- 1 tsp vinegar
- 1 tsp mustard
- Some fresh, finely chopped tarragon, parsley and chives

Combine panko, salt and pepper in a shallow dish. Place flour in another shallow dish. Beat the eggs in a bowl. Cover fish first in the flour. Dip in egg mixture, and cover in panko mixture. Pour the oil in a preheated non-stick skillet. Cook the fish in batches for about 4 minutes until golden and cooked through. Delicious with fresh tartar sauce!

For the light tartar sauce: combine all ingredients.

SPINACH & GOAT CHEESE QUICHE

Adjust oven rack to middle position and preheat to 400°F. Roll out pie dough and place in a 9 ½ inch frypan. Gently prick pie dough all over with a fork making sure that you don't fully puncture the dough. Cover with foil, weight down with pie weights. Place in the oven and bake until browned, about 15 minutes. Remove from oven and reserve.

Meanwhile, melt butter in a medium skillet over medium high heat. Add onion and cook, stirring, until beginning to brown, about 4 minutes. Add drained spinach and season with salt and pepper to taste. Transfer spinach mixture to pie crust. Whisk together eggs and milk then pour over spinach mixture. Press goat cheese chunks into the quiche. Make sure everything is covered with egg mixture.

Place in the oven and bake until quiche is puffy and beginning to brown in spots, about 35 minutes. Allow to cool for 10 minutes and get the quich out of the pan for slicing and serving.

- 1 pie crust (ready made)
- 2 tbsp butter
- 1 small onion (finely chopped)
- 10 oz frozen spinach
  (thawed and squeezed of all excess liquid)
- 5 eggs (beaten)
- ¼ cup milk
- ½ cup fresh goat cheese
- Salt and black pepper

- 2 tbsp olive oil
- 1 zucchini (shredded)
- ½ red bell pepper (finely chopped)
- 1 small red onion (thinly sliced)
- 2 garlic cloves (minced)
- 1 tsp ground cumin
- ¼ cup chopped fresh cilantro
- 1 large tomato (seeded and chopped)
- Juice of 1 lime
- ¼ tsp hot pepper sauce
- 4 whole wheat or white flower tortillas
- 2 cups shredded Monterey Jack cheese
- Salt and pepper

20 MIN

141

ZUCCHINI QUESADILLAS

Heat the oil in a skillet over medium heat. Add the zucchini, bell pepper, onion, garlic and cumin. Cook for 5 minutes, or until all the vegetables are soft. Stir in the cilantro, salt, and pepper. Set aside. In a small bowl, combine the tomato, lime juice, chili powder and hot pepper sauce. Spread ¼ of the zucchini-mixture evenly over half of each tortilla. Sprinkle each with ¼ of the cheese. Fold the tortillas in half. In a large frying pan, cook the quesadillas for about 5 minutes, turning once, until the cheese is melted. Cut the quesadillas into wedges and serve with the tomato mixture.

CHICKEN POT PIES

Preheat the oven to 400°F. Heat the oil in a large saucepan. Add the mushrooms and onion and cook over medium heat, stirring frequently for 7 minutes. Add the chicken cubes, carrots, celery and half the stock and bring to a boil. Reduce the heat and simmer for 12 minutes, until the vegetables are almost tender.

Melt the butter in a large saucepan over medium heat. Whisk in the flour and cook, stirring continuously, for 4 minutes. Gradually beat in the remaining stock. Simmer, stirring, until thick. Stir in the vegetable mixture, chicken, peas and thyme. Simmer for another 5 minutes. Season to taste with salt and pepper. Divide the mixture among six ramekins.

Roll out the dough on a floured surface and cut out 6 circles (1 inch larger than the ramekins). Place the dough circles on top of the filling and crimp the edges. Cut a small cross in the centers. Bake the ramekins in the oven for 15 minutes at 400°F until golden brown.

40 MIN · 6 ·

- 1 tbsp peanut oil
- 3 cups sliced mushrooms
- 1 onion (finely chopped)
- 5 carrots (sliced)
- 1 ¼ cups chicken stock
- 4 tbsp butter
- ½ cup all-purpose flour
- 2 lb chicken breasts
  (1 inch cubes)
- ¾ cup frozen peas
- 1 tsp chopped fresh thyme
- 2 sheets rolled dough pie crusts
- 1 egg (lightly beaten)
- Salt and pepper

RATATOUILLE

Slice eggplants lengthwise, sprinkle with salt, and leave for 1 hour to draw out any bitter juices. Rinse well and pat dry. Slice onions into rings. Cut tomatoes in half and discard seeds. Cut the tomato-flesh into chunks. Peel garlic cloves and crush them. Heat 2 tbsp of olive oil in a sauce pan and cook onions and garlic for 7 minutes until soft. Add tomatoes, bay leaf, rosemary sprigs and basil, pepper and salt and cook for 15 minutes, raising the heat to evaporate any excess juices. Remove from heat and let cool slightly.

Cut the red peppers lengthwise into four, discarding the seeds. Cut each zucchini lengthwise into fine slices, discarding the outer slices. Brush eggplant, red pepper and zucchini with olive oil and grill on the grill pan until cooked and marked. Layer eggplant and red pepper, then tomato stew, more red pepper, eggplant and zucchini, finishing with a dollop of tomato stew, some crumbled goat cheese, a rosemary sprig and a leaf of basil. Serve hot or cold.

20 MIN

- · 2 eggplants
- · 3 onions
- · 6 tomatoes
- · 2 garlic cloves
- · 2 tbsp olive oil
- · 1 bay leaf
- · 4 sprigs rosemary
- · Small bunch of basil
- · 2 red bell peppers
- · 3 zucchini
- · ½ cup fresh goat cheese (crumbled)
- · Salt and pepper

MUSSELS FROM BRUSSELS

- 8 lbs of fresh mussels
- 1 cup white wine (optional)
- 2 white onions
- 5 garlic cloves (to taste)
- 3 carrots
- 1 leek
- 3 celery stalks and leaves
- Salt and pepper

As a general rule, count on about 2 pounds of mussels per person. First, rinse the mussels three or four times in cold water, letting them soak for a couple of minutes to remove sand and silt. The shells that aren't already open should open slightly under water. Scrape off any barnacles attached to the shells.

Throw all the bite-size chopped vegetables into a large pot with a little water (or white wine) at the bottom and set on a low to medium heat. The last thing to do is add the mussels, as they generally only take a few minutes to cook, depending on their size.

Once the veggies have softened, add the mussels to the pot, turn up the heat to high and sprinkle with salt and pepper. Cover and bring to a boil. Pick up the pot a few times and give it a good shake. Once the mussels are all open and their flesh is firm but still juicy, place the whole steaming pot on the table and serve with french fries and mayonnaise or sliced baguette.

20 MIN

DESSERTS

ZABAIONE

Place the egg yolks, sugar and liquids in a saucepan and whisk for about 1 minute. Place the saucepan on the stovetop on low heat. Beat vigorously for about 7-10 minutes.

When it starts to foam, raise the heat and whisk until thick, creamy and foamy. Immediately pour into serving glasses. Serve with some Italian biscotti or amaretti cookies.

· 4 egg yolks

· 4 tbsp granulated sugar

· 4 tbsp white wine

· 2 tbsp amaretto

ORANGE PAN—TART

Preheat the oven to 320°F. To make the topping, place the sugar, water and vanilla in a 9.5 inch non-stick ovenproof frying pan over medium heat. Stir until the sugar is dissolved.

Add the orange slices and simmer for 10-15 minutes or until the orange is soft. Remove from the heat and set aside. Mix eggs, sugar and vanilla with an electric mixer and whisk for 8-10 minutes or until the mixture is thick and pale.

Sift the flour over the egg mixture and fold through. Fold through the butter and almond meal. Pour the mixture over the orange slices and bake for 40-45 minutes or until cooked when tested with a skewer. Turn out onto a platter to serve.

For the topping

- ½ cup caster (superfine) sugar
- ½ cup water
- 1 vanilla bean (split and seeds scraped)
- 2 oranges (very thinly sliced)

For the cake

- 4 eggs
- 1 cup caster (superfine) sugar
- 1 tsp vanilla extract
- 1 ¼ cup self-rising flour
- ½ cup butter (melted)
- 1 cup almond meal
(ground almonds)

GINGERBREAD MEN

Preparation method: Sift together the flour, baking soda, ginger and cinnamon and pour into the bowl of a food processor. Add the butter and blend. Stir in the sugar. Lightly beat the egg and golden syrup together, add to the food processor and mix. Tip the dough out, knead briefly until smooth, wrap in clingfilm and leave to chill in the fridge for 15 minutes.

Icing to decorate: Combine 1 cup sifted powdered sugar and 1 tablespoon water. Spoon the mixture into a zip-top plastic bag. Snip a very small hole off the corner of the bag.

Preheat the oven to 350°F. Roll the dough out to a ¼ inch thickness on a lightly floured surface. Using cutters, cut out the gingerbread men shapes and place on the baking tray, leaving a gap between them. Bake for 12-15 minutes, or until lightly golden-brown. Leave on the tray for 10 minutes and then move to a wire rack to finish cooling. When cooled decorate with the writing icing.

60 MIN · 141 ·

- 3 cups plain flour
- 1 tsp baking soda
- 2 tsp ground ginger
- 1 tsp ground cinnamon
- ½ cup butter
- ¾ cup light soft brown sugar
- 1 free-range egg
- 4 tbsp golden syrup or molasses

CREAM TARTS

Put the flour in a large mixing bowl and whisk in ¼ cup of cream. Pour the rest of the cream in a saucepan, add the lemon zest and vanilla seeds & pod (Split the pod lengthwise into two halves and scrape the pod halves. You add the seeds and the pod to the liquid). Warm slightly (do not boil!) on medium high heat.

Pour the hot cream into the flour mixture along with the sugar and stir well. Add the egg yolks and stir. Put the contents of the bowl back into the saucepan and warm up to boil, meanwhile, continue to stir well.

When it has thickened, remove the pot from the heat and let cool. Remove the lemon zest. Put 2 sheets of puff pastry together and roll them loosely. Cut discs about 1 ½ inch. Press the disks flat and make a 'bowl' out of them. Put them in the muffin pan. Fill the bowls with the cooled cream filling and place in a preheated oven at 420°F for 20 min.

· 1 ¼ cups whipping cream

· 2 puff pastry sheets

· 4 egg yolks

· ¾ cups granulated sugar

· Lemon zest of ½ lemons

· ¼ cup all purpose flour

· 1 vanilla bean

CHEESECAKE

Preheat your oven to 350°F. Place first 5 ingredients in a large bowl; beat with a mixer at medium speed for 2 minutes or until smooth. Add eggs, 1 at a time, beating well after each addition.

Pour batter into a 10-inch springform pan coated with butter. Mix in 2 handfuls of raspberries. Bake at 350°F for 1 hour or until cheesecake center barely moves when pan is touched.

Remove cheesecake from oven; run a knife around the outside edge of cheesecake. Cool slightly; remove outer ring from pan. Garnish with some extra raspberries.

  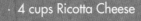

- 4 cups Ricotta Cheese
- 1 cup granulated sugar
- 1 tbsp grated lemon rind
- 2 tsp vanilla extract
- ¼ tsp salt
- 4 large eggs
- 2 cups raspberries
- Butter to grease

STRAWBERRY YOGURT CAKE

Preheat oven to 350°F. Butter and flour a square baking pan. Combine the lemon zest, sugar and butter in a mixer and mix until fluffy, about 3 minutes. Add the eggs and beat until incorporated, about 3 more minutes. Beat in the yogurt, cream and lemon juice.

In a separate bowl, whisk together the flour, baking powder, baking soda and salt. Mix into the dry ingredients, stirring just until fully incorporated. Pour into prepared baking pan and smooth the top.

Arrange the halved berries on top of the cake, cut-side down. Bake 30-35 minutes, or until a tester inserted in the center of the cake comes out clean. Serve sprinkled with powdered sugar, if desired.

60 MIN | 6

- · 1 tsp fresh grated lemon zest
- · 1 cup granulated white sugar
- · ½ cup unsalted butter (softened)
- · 2 large eggs
- · 1 cup Greek yogurt
- · ¼ cup cream
- · 1 tbsp lemon juice
- · 2 cups all purpose flour
- · 1 tsp baking powder
- · 1 tsp baking soda
- · 1 tsp salt
- · 1 pint strawberries
  (washed, hulled, and sliced in half)

- 1 sheet puff pastry
- ¾ cup superfine sugar
- ¼ cup water
- ¼ cup unsalted butter (chopped)
- 5 apples (peeled, cored and quartered)

60 MIN ⑪61

TARTE TATIN

Preheat oven to 375°F. Place the sugar and water in a 9.5 inch round non-stick frying pan over low heat and cook, stirring, until the sugar is dissolved. Increase the heat to medium and bring to a boil. Cook, without stirring, for 7–9 minutes or until lightly golden. Carefully add the butter and stir until melted and well combined. Remove the pan from the heat and carefully arrange the apple, cut-side up and slightly overlapping, in the caramel. Top the apple with the pastry round and fold the edges under to tuck in the apples. Using a fork, make a few marks in the center of the pastry. Bake for 35–40 minutes or until the pastry is puffed and golden. Allow to stand for 2–3 minutes. Carefully turn out the tart to serve.

MARBLED HAZELNUT POUND CAKE

Heat oven to 350°F. Grease a cake tin with a bit of butter. Beat the butter and sugar together, then add the eggs, one at a time, mixing well after each addition. Fold through the sifted flour, milk and vanilla extract until the mixture is smooth.

Divide the mixture between 2 bowls. Stir the cocoa powder and some hazelnuts into the mixture in one of the bowls. Take 2 spoons and use them to dollop the chocolate and vanilla cake mixes into the tin alternately.

Take a skewer and swirl it around the mixture in the tin a few times to create a marbled effect. Top with hazelnuts. Bake the cake for 45-55 minutes until a skewer inserted into the center of the cake comes out clean. After 5 minutes turn out onto a cooling rack and leave to cool.

70 MIN · ¶¶¶ 161

- ¾ cup butter (softened)
- ¾ cup caster sugar
- 3 eggs
- 1 ¼ cup self-rising flour
- 2 tbsp milk
- 1 tsp vanilla extract
- 1 tbsp cocoa powder
- 1 cup chopped hazelnuts

CHOCOLATE MUFFINS

Preheat the oven to 400°F. Combine the flour, baking powder and salt. Melt the butter. Beat the eggs in a separate bowl and then add the sugar, milk and vanilla to the eggs. Thoroughly grease and flour a muffin pan or use paper muffin liners.

Pour a tiny bit of the melted butter into the egg-vanilla-milk mixture and stir it in. Repeat 3-4 more times, adding a slightly larger amount of the liquid butter each time until it is all incorporated. Mix in the dark chocolate chips. Add the liquid ingredients to the dry ones and mix shortly.

Gently pour the batter into the prepared muffin pan or liners and bake immediately. Bake 20 minutes or until a toothpick inserted into the center of a muffin comes out clean.

- 2 cups all-purpose flour
- ½ cup granulated sugar
- 1 tbsp baking powder
- ½ tsp salt
- 1 cup whole milk
- 1 tsp pure vanilla extract
- 2 eggs
- 4 tbsp butter (½ stick)
- ½ cup dark chocolate chips

LEMON TART

For the tart crust: place the flour, butter and icing sugar in the bowl of a food processor and mix. Add the egg yolks and mix to combine. Add the iced water and mix until the dough just comes together. Turn dough out onto a lightly floured surface and form a ball. Wrap in plastic wrap and refrigerate for 1 hour.

Preheat oven to 350°F. Roll the pastry out between 2 sheets of non-stick baking paper. Line a greased tart tin with the pastry, trim the edges and prick the base with a fork. Refrigerate for 30 minutes. Line the pastry case with baking paper and fill with baking beans. Bake for 15 minutes, remove the paper and baking beans and bake for a further 10 minutes. Reduce temperature to 275°F.

To make the lemon filling: place the cream, eggs, extra yolks, sugar and lemon juice in a bowl and whisk to combine. Pour into the baked tart shell. Bake for 30–35 minutes at 350°F. Allow to cool and refrigerate until completely set.

For the tart crust

- 1½ cups plain all-purpose flour
- ½ cup chilled butter (cut into cubes)
- 3 egg yolks
- 1 tbsp iced water

lemon filling

- 1 cup single (pouring) cream
- 2 eggs
- 3 egg yolks, extra
- ½ cup caster sugar
- ½ cup lemon juice

85

RASPBERRY AND WHITE CHOCOLATE MUFFINS

Preheat the oven to 400°F. Chop the chocolate into large chunks. Sift the flour and the baking powder into a large bowl. Stir the sugar into the flour mixture. In a separate bowl crack the eggs. Whisk in the vanilla extract, melted butter and milk. Stir the two mixtures together.

Carefully fold in the raspberries and white chocolate. Ladle batter into a greased muffin tray. Bake for 20 minutes. Let cool in pan for 5 minutes, tip out muffins and let cool completely.

- 1¾ cup all-purpose flour
- 2 tsp baking powder
- ½ cup granulated sugar
- 3 eggs
- 1 tsp vanilla extract
- ½ cup milk
- ½ cup butter
- ¾ cup raspberries
- ¾ cup white chocolate

PECAN PANCAKES

Stir together the first 8 ingredients until well combined. Whisk together buttermilk, oil, and egg in a bowl; add to the flour mixture and stir. Pour a small ladle of batter for each pancake onto a hot, lightly greased large skillet.

Cook the pancakes 2 to 3 minutes. Turn and cook the other sides. Top with some pecan nuts and maple syrup. Serve immediately.

15 MIN | 41

- 1 cup all-purpose flour
- ⅓ cup pecans (toasted)
- 1 tsp granulated sugar
- 1 tsp light brown sugar
- ½ tsp baking powder
- ½ tsp ground cinnamon
- ¼ tsp baking soda
- ⅛ tsp salt
- 1 cup nonfat buttermilk
- 1 tbsp peanut oil
- 1 large egg
- Maple syrup

89

- 2 tbsp butter
- ½ cup dark chocolate
- ⅛ cup sugar
- ¼ cup cream
- 2 egg yolks
- 4 egg whites
- White chocolate shavings
- Some fresh mint leaves

CHOCOLATE MOUSSE

Break the dark chocolate into small pieces and melt slowly on very low heat in a saucepan. Remove from the heat and whisk in the egg yolk. In a large bowl, whisk the egg whites until they form soft peaks.

Carefully fold the egg whites into the melted chocolate. Pour into 4 serving bowls and chill in the fridge for at least one hour. Top with the white chocolate shavings and a mint leaf.

- 4 cups bread (pulled apart)
- ¾ cup sugar
- 2 cups raisins
- 1 ¼ cups milk
- 5 tbsp butter (plus extra for lining the tin)
- 2 tsp mixed spice
- 1 tsp vanilla extract

RAISIN BREAD PUDDING

Preheat the oven to 350°F. In a large casserole, lightly heat the milk, butter, fruit and sugar. Mix in the teared apart bread slices, mixed spice and vanilla, stir well. Grease a roasting tin and fill with the mixture, spread well into all corners. Cover with a piece of foil so the raisins do not burn (remove this 10 minutes before end of cooking time). Bake for 45-55 minutes or until golden brown.

70 MIN

161

HEALTHY COOKING HAS A NAME: GREENPAN™

In 2007, GreenPan™ brought about a genuine revolution in the kitchen. The Belgian kitchenware brand uses Thermolon™, a patented ceramic non-stick coating which is completely free of PFAS, PFOA, lead and cadmium for its comprehensive range of pots and pans. This new technology guarantees effortless cooking, great non-stick and an easy clean-up. Chefs and foodies are already convinced of the benefits. Want to bet you'll be next?

· Thermolon™ Ceramic non-stick coating:
  100% free of PFAS, PFOA, Lead and Cadmium
· Long-lasting: the non-stick layer will not peel
  off or break down as a result of overheating
· The even heat distribution guarantees perfect results
· Easy to use when both cooking and cleaning

The Original
GREEN PAN™

CARE AND USE

Healthy cooking is not only about the foods you use: it is also about the right cookware! GreenPan™ has made a real revolution in the non-stick cookware market, producing a new generation of cookware that is safe and convenient for use.

The core of GreenPan™ is the patented ceramic non-stick coating used on all non-stick products. Thermolon™ was the first of its kind, the original ceramic non-stick coating on the market, ever.

Thermolon™ is a non-stick coating with excellent thermal conductivity which allows perfect frying results with lower heat settings than traditional non-stick coatings. The coating is also highly scratch-resistant, very hard and more resistant to thermal shocks.

Tips-and-Tricks for healthy and happy cooking in GreenPan™

Heat settings

GreenPan™ cookware, unlike traditional non-stick, can withstand high temperatures, but low to medium heat works best! Why? This is because the Thermolon ceramic non-stick coating conducts heat extremely well, so food tends to fry faster.

Please take note, short high heat can be used for searing and browning, but continual high heat can eventually burn fats and cause build up. To preserve the functionality of your cookware, low to medium heat is perfect!

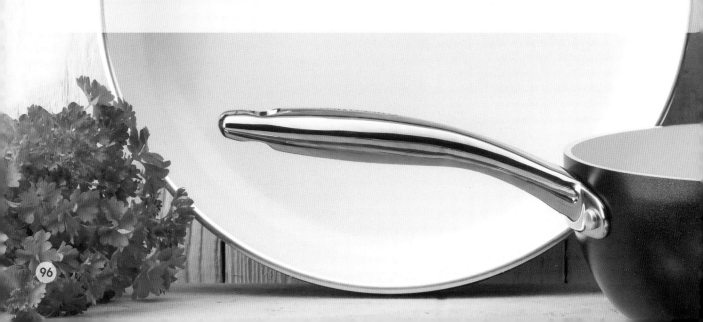

Oils

Oils are a great addition to any dish! When using fats and oils with your GreenPan™, be sure to check their smoke point (For example, Extra Virgin Olive Oil has a low smoke point and should be used on lower temperatures, where oils such as safflower and corn have high smoke points and can be used on higher heat.) However, please avoid using any type of spray oil. The tiny droplets can carbonize very quickly and will cause sticking issues.

Handling the pan

Wooden, bamboo, silicone, nylon...all of these types of utensils are completely safe to use on your GreenPan™. Since Thermolon™ is a coating, we ask you avoid metal utensils, so accidental scratching won't occur. Also, make sure to keep an eye on your food as it cooks! Because ceramic coatings tend to heat faster, unattended food can burn.

Cleaning & storing

Please allow your cookware to cool completely before washing. A hot pan in cold water can result in a thermal shock and eventually deform your frypan.

Hand washing is always recommended for all GreenPan™ cookware. Please chek your specific care and use for further details on your collection.

Make sure your cookware is clean before storing. When storing and stacking pans inside of each other, a protective sheet helps to keep your cookware looking just like new!